Media Analysis Tools

For Selecting the Proper Periodicals
for the Advertising Schedule

R. L. Ehler

RICHLER & CO.
Santa Barbara, CA 93105 U.S.A.

Media Analysis Tools
For Selecting the Proper Periodicals for the Advertising Schedule
By R.L. Ehler

Published by Richler & Co.
754 Palermo Dr., Ste. A
Santa Barbara, CA 93105, U.S.A.
Phone (805) 569-1668
FAX (805) 569-2279

Library of Congress Catalog Card No.: 90-63639

Publisher's Cataloging in Publication
(Prepared by Quality Books Inc.)

Ehler, R.L. (Richard Lee), 1930-
    Media   analysis   tools : for   selecting   the   proper   periodicals   for   the
advertising   schedule / R.L. Ehler.--
    p. cm--(Print media advertising series ; book 3)
    ISBN 1-87929-913-5
    1. Advertising media planning. 2. Advertising, Magazine--Handbooks, manuals, etc.
 3. Advertising, Newspaper--Handbooks, manuals, etc. I. Title. II. Series

HF6107   659.132
                                                         QB90-11
                                                         MARC

The Print Media Advertising Series

This book is one of a series published by Richler & Co. The Print Media Advertising Series provides timely, practical information about media planning and buying functions to help the appropriate persons in businesses that advertise as well as those in their advertising agencies.

Books published in this series:

The Print Media Planning Manual: How to Prepare a Media Plan and Buy Space for Periodical Advertising
by R.L. Ehler

Directory of Print Media Advertising Resources: Nearly 400 Sources for Facts and Figures Needed By the Print Media Planner and Buyer
by R.L. Ehler

Media Analysis Tools: For Selecting the Proper Periodicals for the Advertising Schedule
by R.L. Ehler

Checklists for Print Media Advertising Planning and Buying: 13 Basic Checklists, 195 Specific Things to Check When Planning and Buying Advertising in Periodicals
by R.L. Ehler

ABOUT THE AUTHOR

R.L. Ehler has more than 30 years in the marketing communications field, having been at various times in his career an advertising agency co-owner and vice president, account executive, media planner and buyer, copywriter, advertising manager, magazine and newspaper editor, and market planner.

His experience has been on both the agency and advertiser side and covers all media. He has worked on industrial, consumer and retail accounts, including electronics; travel/destination; food; land development; furniture; apparel and shopping centers; transportation; material handling; machine tools; water treatment; oil and gas exploration and production; agriculture; construction materials; and schools. His articles on advertising planning and media selection have appeared in trade magazines both in the United States and abroad.

He was prompted to write this book because so many of his colleagues, noting his unique experience and ability to organize and simplify complex subjects, approached him to share his insight into how the media selection process can be systematized. The result is a book that will save the media planner countless hours of time and effort in selecting the proper periodicals for the advertising schedule.

TABLE OF CONTENTS

DISCLAIMER

This book is designed to provide information on selecting periodicals for the advertising schedule. It is sold with the understanding that neither the publisher nor the author, through this book, is rendering legal, accounting or other professional services. If such expert assistance is required, the reader should seek the services of an appropriate professional.

It is not the purpose of this book to present all the information that is otherwise available to the author and/or publisher but to compliment, amplify and supplement other texts and to present an approach which the author has found to be useful in selecting the proper periodicals for the advertising schedule.

Periodical selection is a function that requires an investment in time and effort before any degree of proficiency can be achieved.

Every effort has been made to make this book as thorough and accurate as possible. However, there may be omissions or mistakes both typographical and in content. Thus, the text should be used only as a general guide and not as the only source on periodical selection for the advertising schedule. Additionally, this book contains information on the subject up to the printing date.

The author and Richler & Co. shall have neither liability nor responsibility to any person or organization with respect to any loss or damage caused or alleged to be caused directly or indirectly by the information contained in this book.

INTRODUCTION

People who plan advertising campaigns and buy the space in periodicals have never had a greater selection of publications from which to choose. There are over 6,000 business publications and over 2,200 consumer publications in the U.S. vying for advertisers' money each year. Farm publications in the U.S. total over 700. Daily newspapers total some 1650 in the U.S. Telephone directories with their advertising sections are to be found virtually in every town in America.

And then there are overseas publications. More than 750 major new publications started up in Western Europe alone in one recent year.

Within a given field of interest to the advertiser, there may be 20, even 30,50,70 different periodicals vying for a spot on the advertising schedule.

Given the plethora of periodicals serving the print advertiser's interests, how can the media planner decide with any degree of confidence which ones to put on the schedule?

The purpose of this book is to provide a set of tools to assist in carrying out the selection process. The tools have been designed to allow you to measure and compare on a numerical basis each of the various attributes of the contending periodicals and then to arrive at an overall ranking of each periodical's effectiveness in reaching your prospects.

The media analysis tools can be used by small and large advertisers alike to quickly yet systematically select the proper publications for a given situation. There is a tool for each of the 15 key measurement categories that must be analyzed in order to make sound decisions concerning media selection.

The tools are in the form of calculations and tables for each of the 15 key measurement categories. The calculations are used to arrive at weighted scores for each of the contending periodicals. The tables are used to evaluate each periodical on a weighted and non-weighted basis. Summary tables present the total scores--and thus ranking--for all of the periodicals being considered for the advertising schedule.

Note that while the tools which follow have been developed specifically for use with the aforementioned 15 key measurement categories, with minor modification they may also be used to measure other secondary attributes, such as frequency of issue, age of periodical, field editorial network, etc.

CHAPTER 1

PREPARATION FOR USING TOOLS

Before using the media analysis tools, the media planner must acquire certain facts about each of the periodicals serving the advertiser's field of interest. These facts center around circulation, editorial, use by industry advertisers, inquiry performance, and cost considerations.

Some of these facts can be obtained from standard source references, such as Standard Rate and Data Service. Other facts will require contacting media representatives. examining issues of the periodicals serving the field, etc. The reader is advised to send for copies of Print Media Planning Manual and Directory of Print Media Advertising Resources, both available from Richler & Co. (see Order Form in the back of this book). The manual provides a basic grounding on the subject of print media planning in general. It examines in great detail all of the considerations that go into preparing a media plan and buying the space for periodical advertising, including expansive discussions on the facts about publications which are needed in order to use the media analysis tools. The directory lists the names, addresses and telephone numbers of virtually every important source for facts and figures about periodicals available to the advertiser, both in the United State and abroad.

NOTE: Whether or not the reader uses the manual and directory as aids in acquiring the necessary background and facts about the periodicals, acquisition by whatever means of ALL needed input for EACH publication serving the given field is absolutely essential to make the tools in this book work properly.

CHAPTER 2

THE 15 KEY MEASUREMENT CATEGORIES

The 15 key measurement categories, or factors, to be comparatively analyzed periodical by periodical cover circulation, editorial, use by industry's advertisers, inquiry performance, and cost considerations. They are as follows:

1. Total Circulation
2. Paid Circulation
3. Audited Circulation
4. Geographic Circulation
5. Circulation by Activity--
   a. Business Circulation by Industry Type (for business magazines)
   b. Demographic Circulation (for consumer magazines and newspapers)
6. Occupation/Job Function Circulation (for business magazines)
7. Editorial Coverage of Industry or Field
8. Advertising Makeup
9. Editorial Makeup
10. Number of Editorial Awards
11. Editors With Industry-Related Degrees and/or Work Experience
12. Reader Service Cards Processed (for magazines)
13. Advertising Inquiries Received (for magazines)
14. General Editorial Inquiries Received (for magazines)
15. Cost Per Thousand

1.   TOTAL CIRCULATION

The preferred source for the total circulation figures, as with all other input pertaining to circulation considerations, should be the audited statement of circulation. If such a statement is not available from the publisher, the publisher's sworn statement of circulation may be used.

Note that the audited statement will present two sets of figures for total circulation--an averaged total for the six months covered by the statement and a total for the last issue published during the six months being reported. Use the latter figure UNLESS the totals for each of the six months show volatile activity, in which case you should use the averaged total figure.

On the surface, a periodical's total circulation would appear to be the most important consideration for the advertiser. Indeed, it is important, but other factors about its circulation need to be examined, as we shall see.

2.   PAID CIRCULATION

Are subscriptions sold or given at no charge? There are periodicals that are totally one way or the other. And there are some that offer a mix--some copies are paid for, others are given free of charge. As with most of the other measurement categories, it will be the media planner's responsibility to assign a value to this consideration.

3.   AUDITED CIRCULATION

Publishers must deliver X number of readers in order to justify a given advertising rate. An audit of the publication's circulation is the advertiser's independent assurance that the periodical will deliver its claimed readers.

The audited statement defines the kinds of people the periodical reaches within a field. It verifies currency of names, breaks out occupations, gives the geographic location of recipients, checks for duplication, validates printing invoices, confirms postal receipts, and actually tests a selection of the names on the list.

4.   GEOGRAPHIC CIRCULATION

Those publishers that have national circulation should be able to provide a state by state breakdown tied to the appropriate zip codes. The state by state presentation will usually be grouped into regions--e.g., New England, Middle Atlantic, Mountain, Pacific, etc.

In the case of newspapers, circulation figures should be available by city, retail trading and primary market zones. The circulation may also be available by area of dominant influence (ADI), designated market area (DMA), or metropolitan statistical area (MSA).

5. CIRCULATION BY ACTIVITY

Business publications will present circulation broken down by primary and secondary end product or service. This breakdown will usually be accompanied by Standard Industrial Classification (SIC) numbers as a further assist to the media planner. The SIC system is the U.S. Government's way of classifying the country's entire field of economic activities, with each activity being assigned both a group number and an industry number.

Consumer magazines and newspapers will present their circulation demographically--that is, by number of households, gross household income, number of men and women, age, etc.

6. OCCUPATION/JOB FUNCTION CIRCULATION

Circulation of the business magazine needs to be examined by occupation and job title. The broadest classification, of course, is occupation--e.g., engineering. The job function performed or job title held helps to pin down the readers' specific areas of responsibility--e.g., chief engineer, process engineer, or engineering manager.

7. EDITORIAL COVERAGE OF INDUSTRY OR FIELD

This measurement category has to do with the total number of editorial pages devoted to the advertiser's industry or field of interest in general. An example of a general field would be travel, as opposed to lodging which is a segment of the travel industry. Travel, in the broader sense, encompasses transportation, recreational activities, scenic attractions, dining facilities, lodging accommodations, etc.

8. ADVERTISING MAKEUP

This measurement category narrows the industry/field to the advertiser's specific interests. This category hones in on the number of advertisements by unit size which have appeared during the past six or twelve months (media planner's choice) which advertised the same product or service as that of the advertiser's. What the comparisons in this category provide is an indication of how important the advertiser's competition regards the periodicals' readers for the products/services they are advertising.

9. EDITORIAL MAKEUP

Similarly, this category presents the number of editorial pages that are devoted over time to the advertiser's type of product or service. The volume serves as a clear indication of whether the periodical serves the field in which the advertiser is interested in reaching with his advertising message.

The publishers should be able to provide such an accounting by general product or service category. They may even compare their counts with those of their competition's. To get these counts, though, the media planner may have to have his or her own counts made. The same holds true for competing ad page counts.

10. NUMBER OF EDITORIAL AWARDS

How many awards for editorial excellence in its field has the publication and its editors garnered? This consideration serves as a measure of the publication's standing in journalistic achievement in serving its field of interest. Well written publications that do outstanding work in reporting tend to be among the best read publications in their field.

Having said this, be cognizant of the probability that the counts in this category will be low. Some industries don't offer such honors nor do some publications put much stock in competing for awards. Still, it should be interesting to see where the counts fall.

11. EDITORS WITH INDUSTRY-RELATED DEGREES AND/OR WORK EXPERIENCE

Having editors who have been trained by formal education and work experience in the field the publication addresses helps the editors perform their editorial duties and is a plus for the publication. This is particularly true if the field served is highly technical or scientific. Certainly it can be argued, for example, that having a medical degree is helpful in performing editorial duties for a medical journal or periodical.

In non-technical fields, x number of years of "hands-on" work experience may be viewed as being equal to the training received in an educational institution. It is suggested, for purposes of arriving at comparative measurements in this category, that 10 years would be an acceptable substitute for a degree in non-technical fields.

12. READER SERVICE CARDS PROCESSED

Most business magazines and many consumer magazines offer their readers a convenient means of obtaining more information about the products or services mentioned in advertisements and articles. The reader service card, or bingo card, is the most commonly used vehicle to achieve this purpose. A card is stitched into the issue onto which has been printed a series of numbers. Each of these numbers corresponds to a like number which has been imprinted at the bottom of a story or advertisement in the issue. If the reader wants more information on the product or service covered in the story or advertisement, he or she circles the appropriate number on the card, fills in his or her name and address and mails the card to the magazine. The magazine notifies the story source or advertiser that the reader has requested additional information.

13. ADVERTISING INQUIRIES RECEIVED

The magazine should be able to break out from the total number of inquiries received from all sources the total number of inquiries received from all advertisements in the magazine's issues. The latter figure is the basis for comparison in this measurement category. Note that the advertiser may wish to add to that figure the number of inquiries traceable to the magazine which bypass the bingo card system and go directly to the advertiser. Examples of such bypass avenues are telemarketing toll free 800 numbers and correspondence on company letterhead.

14.   GENERAL EDITORIAL INQUIRIES RECEIVED

Likewise, the magazine should be able to break out from the total number of inquiries received those which are as a result of editorial coverage. And the media planner may wish to add to that total the inquiries sent by readers directly to the advertiser.

15.   COST PER THOUSAND

Cost per thousand is based on the black and white full run page rate divided by total circulation--e.g., the black and white full run page rate of $3150 divided by 24,866 total readers equals $126.68 per thousand readers. That's what it would cost to reach a thousand readers of the periodical one time with the advertiser's message.

CHAPTER 3

INSTRUCTIONS

TOTAL CIRCULATION

An example of the basic presentation format and scoring technique to be used for each measurement category is shown in Table 1. It shows the ranking (non-weighted and weighted) as it pertains to total circulation of each of eight contending periodicals serving the offshore oil industry. In the example, periodical A ranks first both on a non-weighted and weighted basis.

TABLE 1. TOTAL CIRCULATION

Weighting: <u>10 points</u>
Weighted Use Example: 4 (non-weighted ranking) x 10 points = 40 (as in Periodical E's case)

	Actual Circulation	Non-Weighted Ranking	Weighted Ranking
Periodical A	53,603	1	10
Periodical B	44,489	2	20
Periodical C	27,103	5	50
Periodical D	21,130	6	60
Periodical E	28,734	4	40
Periodical F	35,426	3	30
Periodical G	19,100	7	70
Periodical H	15,200	8	80

Note: The fewer the points in ranking the higher the rating--e.g., a ranking of 1 (non-wieghted) and 10 (weighted) is the highest rating.

This same approach as far as basic presentation format and scoring technique is concerned is used for each of the other 14 key measurement categories.

Each of the eight periodicals is ranked on a non-weighted and weighted basis on how well each does in each of the 15 measurement categories.

When scoring on a non-weighted basis, the ranking number which shows position among the periodicals as it pertains to circulation volume, etc., (e.g., 1 for the first place periodical, 2 for second place periodical, etc.) becomes the non-weighted score for the periodical in each category. As we shall see shortly, the total of the ranking numbers from all fifteen of the measurement categories is the periodical's total non-weighted score.

Note in Table 1 where it says "Weighting: 10 points." That means that a weighted value of 10 points has been assigned to total circulation as a measurement category. To arrive at the weighted score, each of the measurement categories is assigned a value number of 1, 5, 10 or 15 with number 1 being the highest rating, number 5 being next highest, etc. It is up to the reader to assign his or her own value to each of the 15 measurement categories based on the importance of those categories to his or her own advertising situation. For purposes of illustration, the author has assigned the following values:

<u>Value Points</u>

Total Circulation	10
Paid Circulation	10
Audited Circulation	10
Geographic Circulation	10
Circulation by Activity	5
Occupation/Job Function Circulation	1
Editorial Coverage of Industry or Field	1
Advertising Makeup	10
Editorial Makeup	10
Number of Editorial Awards	15
Editors With Industry-Related Degrees and/or Work Experience	15
Reader Service Cards	15
Advertising Inquiries Received	15
General Editorial Inquiries Received	15
Cost Per Thousand	15

Refer again to Table 1. In the example, Total Circulation has been judged to have a value of 10 points. Each periodical's non-weighted ranking number is multiplied by the value number 10 and the result becomes the weighted score. For example, periodical D's non-weighted score is 6. The assigned value of this category is 10 points. Thus, periodical D's weighted score is 60 (10 X 6).

It is important to remember that in the case of both weighted and non-weighted scoring the lower the number a periodical garners the better the ranking. "Actual" figures (e.g., actual circulation figures) for each of the measurement categories, of course, are the exact opposite--i.e., the higher the number the better the periodical does in that category.

PAID CIRCULATION

Shortly, you will see how each periodical is ranked as to overall effectiveness in coverage according to the total weighted scores achieved from all categories. For now, though, refer to Table 2 which details paid circulation for the hypothetical eight contending periodicals.

TABLE 2. PAID CIRCULATION

Weighting: 10 points
Weighted Use Example: 2 (non-weighted ranking) x 10 points = 20

	Actual Circulation	Non-Weighted Ranking	Weighted Ranking
Periodical A	---	8	80
Periodical B	44,289	1	10
Periodical C	---	8	80
Periodical D	21,130	2	20
Periodical E	14,734	4	40
Periodical F	15,500	3	30
Periodical G	---	8	80
Periodical H	---	8	80

Notes: The fewer the points in ranking the higher the rating--e.g., a ranking of 1 (non-weighted) and 10 (weighted) is the highest rating.

Periodicals having no paid circulation or whose paid circulation figures are not available are assessed the highest number of non-weighted points (8) and the highest number of weighted points (80) for this category.

Four of the eight periodicals are circulated exclusively on a paid basis with periodical B taking first place with a non-weighted score of 1 and a weighted score of 10. The four periodicals that are distributed on a 100% non-paid basis are all penalized to the maximum degree (with 8 non-weighted points and 80 weighted points) because, for purposes of our illustration, it has been determined beforehand that paid circulation is important to the advertising situation.

Note that in the process of penalizing the four non-paid periodicals the maximum amount, there cannot be a fifth, sixth or seventh placed periodical. They each share the eighth or last place position in the rankings.

AUDITED CIRCULATION

The method for treating audited circulation is shown in Table 3.

TABLE 3. AUDITED CIRCULATION

Weighting: <u>10 points</u>
Weighted Use Example: 1 (non-weighted ranking) x 10 points = 10

	Actual	Non-Weighted Ranking	Weighted Ranking
Periodical A	ABC	1	10
Periodical B	BPA	1	10
Periodical C	ABC	1	10
Periodical D	BPA	1	10
Periodical E	BPA	1	10
Periodical F	ABC	1	10
Periodical G	---	8	80
Periodical H	CCAB	1	10

Notes: The fewer the points in ranking the higher the rating--e.g., a ranking of 1 (non-weighted) and 10 (weighted) is the highest rating.

Periodicals which are not audited are assessed the highest number of non-weighted points (8) and the highest number of weighted points (80) for this category.

No attempt is made to place more importance on one type of audit over another. Thus, all periodicals that are audited received the best possible ranking (1 for non-weighted and 10 for weighted).

GEOGRAPHIC CIRCULATION

When measuring geographic circulation, the media planner must decide what segment of geography is important to the advertising situation. The segment(s) involved may center around city, county, state, region, country, or continental considerations. Each segment deemed important would require a separate table for comparisons. Table 4 shows an example of circulation comparisons in the United States. If the advertiser is a multinational company, other tables probably would also be required in order to present worldwide circulation comparisons--e.g., a table each on Africa, Australasis (Australia and Asia), Europe, Canada, Latin America, and Middle East.

22

TABLE 4. GEOGRAPHIC CIRCULATION - U.S.A.

Weighting: <u>10 points</u>
Weighted Use Example: 8 (non-weighted ranking) x 10 points = 80

	Actual	Non-Weighted Ranking	Weighted Ranking
Periodical A	53,000	1	10
Periodical B	43,500	2	20
Periodical C	22,130	4	40
Periodical D	21,090	5	50
Periodical E	14,250	6	60
Periodical F	34,300	3	30
Periodical G	N/A	8	80
Periodical H	---	8	80

Notes: The fewer the points in ranking the higher the rating--e.g., a ranking of 1 (non-weighted) and 10 (weighted) is the highest rating.

NA=circulation figures not available because the periodical is unable to breakout the figures from its totals; periodical is assessed highest number of non-weighted points (8) and highest number of weighted points (80).

--Periodicals which do not have such geographic circulation are assessed the highest number of non-weighted points (8) and the highest number of weighted points (80).

CIRCULATION ACTIVITY

When measuring circulation by activity, the business to business advertiser will be looking at circulation by industry type (Figure 5). The advertiser who is directing his message to consumers will be concerned with demographic circulation. (Figure 6.)

Business publications break their circulation into the SIC economic activities and/or into major groupings by primary end product or service. Table 5 shows an example of a comparison of business periodicals which serve the offshore oil industry.

For purposes of illustrating this particular breakdown, the table shows number of subscribers each periodical has who are in an SIC grouping made up of oil companies, oil company consultants and contract drilling companies. Note: the advertiser's situation may require that the ad message reach more than one particular type of subscriber, in which case a second table, etc., would be required in order to adequately cover circulation be activity. For example, in addition to oil companies, oil company consultants and contract drilling companies, such activities as original equipment manufacturers and fabricators may be of interest to the advertiser.

TABLE 5.   CIRCULATION BY BUSINESS ACTIVITY --
OIL COMPANIES, OIL COMPANY
CONSULTANCIES, CONTRACT DRILLING
COMPANIES

Weighting: 10 points
Weighted Use Example: 4 (non-weighted ranking) x 5 points = 20

	Actual Circulation	Non-Weighted Ranking	Weighted Ranking
Periodical A	39,603	1	5
Periodical B	30,217	2	10
Periodical C	15,200	5	25
Periodical D	16,000	4	20
Periodical E	13,700	6	30
Periodical F	27,254	3	15
Periodical G	13,600	7	35
Periodical H	9,970	8	40

Note: The fewer the points in ranking the higher the rating--e.g., a ranking of 1 (non-weighted) and 5 (weighted) is the highest rating.

Consumer periodicals present their circulation by activity into demographic breakouts, such as number of households, gross household income, number of men and women, age, etc. Just as may be the case with the business-to-business advertiser, a number of tables may be required to cover circulation by activity of contending consumer periodicals. Table 6 shows consumer activity of the periodicals by the advertiser's targeted age group of people 35-54 years old.

TABLE 6. CIRCULATION BY CONSUMER ACTIVITY -- AGE 35-55

Weighting: 5 points
Weighted Use Example: 3 (non-weighted ranking) x 5 points = 15

	Actual Circulation	Non-Weighted Ranking	Weighted Ranking
Periodical A	378,000	4	20
Periodical B	222,190	5	25
Periodical C	540,000	2	10
Periodical D	128,700	6	30
Periodical E	450,000	3	15
Periodical F	781,000	1	5
Periodical G	N/A	8	40
Periodical H	N/A	8	40

Notes: The fewer the points in ranking the higher the rating--e.g., a ranking of 1 (non-weighted) and 5 (weighted) is the highest rating.

NA=Circulation figures not available because the periodical is unable to breakout the figures from its total; periodical is assessed highest number of non-weighted points (8) and highest number of weighted points (40).

OCCUPATION/JOB FUNCTION CIRCULATION

In examining this type of circulation the aim of the media planner is to be able to look at figures that are as specific as possible. Some periodicals, for example, will not be able to breakdown their broader occupation classifications (such as "engineering") by job functions/titles (e.g., "chief engineer"). Those that can and do, though, will fare better in this measurement category. There are, for example, 1,300,000 engineers of all types in the United States. Of that number, only about 46,500 are chemical engineers. The number that are chief chemical engineers is considerably less, and the number of chief chemical engineers who work in water treatment systems manufacturing plants, for example, is a fraction of that. But if the latter is your target and a periodical can pinpoint them in its circulation, you naturally will give serious consideration to including that periodical on the advertising schedule.

Table 7 shows how the group of eight business periodicals fare in reaching design engineers employed in the offshore oil industry. Note that in the example reaching design engineers is considered to be of prime importance--they are assigned a weighted value of 1 point.

TABLE 7. OCCUPATION/JOB FUNCTION CIRCULATION-DESIGN ENGINEERS

Weighting: 1 points
Weighted Use Example: 3 (non-weighted ranking) x 1 point = 3

	Actual Circulation	Non-Weighted Ranking	Weighted Ranking
Periodical A	45,130	1	1
Periodical B	33,605	2	2
Periodical C	N/A	8	8
Periodical D	18,000	4	4
Periodical E	12,400	5	5
Periodical F	21,734	3	3
Periodical G	N/A	8	8
Periodical H	N/A	8	8

Notes: The fewer the points in ranking, the higher the rating--e.g., a ranking of 1 (non-weighted) is the highest rating.

NA=Circulation figures not available because periodical is unable to breakout the figures from its total; periodical is assessed highest number of non-weighted points (8) and highest number of weighted points (8).

In any given advertising situation it is rare that only one occupation or job function is of interest. Usually, there are one or two more that are of interest. For example, the advertiser's prime target may be design engineers but a secondary target may be administrative management (presidents, vice presidents, general managers, department heads) in which case another table of comparisons showing their coverage by periodical would be in order.

EDITORIAL COVERAGE OF INDUSTRY OR FIELD

Next to be compared is the total number of editorial pages devoted to the advertiser's industry or field of interest in general. Later we will measure the number of editorial pages devoted to the advertiser's specific area(s) of interest. The total number of editorial pages devoted to the general subject should cover a period of six or twelve months of issues.

Note: it may very well be that among your contending periodicals there is a mix of weeklies, semi-monthlies and/or bimonthlies. If so, the actual editorial page counts of the weeklies, semi-monthlies and/or bimonthlies must be averaged and adjusted in order to provide a fair comparison of the page counts with those of the monthly periodicals. This applies also to the counts in the tables to be presented later for specific interest editorial and ad pages, reader service cards, ad inquiries and general editorial inquiries.

Table 8 shows total number of editorial pages devoted to the general subject of offshore oil over a given six-month calendar period.

TABLE 8. EDITORIAL COVERAGE OF: OFFSHORE INDUSTRY IN GENERAL

Weighting: 1 point
Weighted Use Example: 4 (non-weighted ranking) x 1 point = 4

	Actual Page Counts	Non-Weighted Ranking	Weighted Ranking
Periodical A	227	4	4
Periodical B	325	1	1
Periodical C	60	8	8
Periodical D	300	2	2
Periodical E	78	7	7
Periodical F	270	3	3
Periodical G	104	6	6
Periodical H	109	5	5

Note: The fewer the points in ranking the higher the rating--e.g., a ranking of 1 (non-weighted) and 1 (weighted) is the highest rating.

An observation on the performance of periodical H in the table: The rankings which periodical H has garnered in all of the table examples leading up to Table 8 would indicate it probably is not going to be a strong contender for the advertising schedule. Note, however, its strong fifth place showing with 109 editorial pages in Table 8. If this is a relative new publication (and for our purposes here we'll say it is), it may be attempting to "buy" into the market by concentrating more editorial attention on the offshore industry than its closest, more mature contenders, periodicals G, E and C. Thus, while it's overall performance may not warrant placing periodical H on the schedule at this time, it deserves to be watched in the future.

ADVERTISING MAKEUP

Table 9 shows a comparison of actual advertising run during the past six months by competing companies of our hypothetical offshore oil industry advertiser. The subjects of the ads were either directly competitive or were generically in the same class as those of our advertiser's.

It is the media planner's choice as to what size display advertising unit is chosen for counting--full page units only, units of one-quarter page or more, etc. If units smaller than full page are included, the media planner must convert these fractionals into the total number of full page units that they represent so that there is a common measurement standard.

TABLE 9. ADVERTISING MAKEUP: OFFSHORE RIG/PLATFORM EQUIPMENT

Weighting: <u>10 points</u>
Weighted Use Example: 2 (non-weighted ranking) x 10 points = 20

	Actual Page Counts	Non-Weighted Ranking	Weighted Ranking
Periodical A	48	4	40
Periodical B	91	1	10
Periodical C	---	8	80
Periodical D	81	2	20
Periodical E	12	5	50
Periodical F	69	3	30
Periodical G	8	6	60
Periodical H	---	8	80

Notes: The fewer the points in ranking the higher the rating--e.g., a ranking of 1 (non-weighted) and 10 (weighted) is the highest rating.

--Periodicals which did not have any advertising running during the six months studied which was pertinent to the media planner's interests are assessed the highest number of non-weighted points (8) and the highest number of weighted points (80).

27

EDITORIAL MAKEUP

Table 10 shows a comparison of actual editorial pages run during the past six months, the subjects of which pertained either directly or generically to our hypothetical offshore oil industry advertiser's products and activities.

TABLE 10. EDITORIAL MAKEUP: OFFSHORE RIG/PLATFORM EQUIPMENT

Weighting: <u>10 points</u>
Weighted Use Example: 5 (non-weighted ranking) x 10 points = 50

	Actual Page Counts	Non-Weighted Ranking	Weighted Ranking
Periodical A	36	4	40
Periodical B	71	2	20
Periodical C	19	6	60
Periodical D	82	1	10
Periodical E	10	7	70
Periodical F	47	3	30
Periodical G	7	8	80
Periodical H	30	5	50

Note: The fewer the points in ranking the higher the rating--e.g., a ranking of 1 (non-weighted) and 10 (weighted) is the highest rating.

NUMBER OF EDITORIAL AWARDS

Table 11 shows number of editorial awards for excellence garnered by the contending periodicals during the previous 12 months. In most cases no awards were recorded either because the periodicals chose not to enter the awards competition or such information was not available to the media planner. Note that those not garnering awards are all penalized to the maximum degree--8 non-weighted and 120 weighted points.

TABLE 11. EDITORIAL AWARDS

Weighting: <u>15 points</u>
Weighted Use Example: 8 (non-weighted ranking) x 15 points = 120

	Actual # Awards	Non-Weighted Ranking	Weighted Ranking
Periodical A	N/A	8	120
Periodical B	1	2	30
Periodical C	3	1	15
Periodical D	---	8	120
Periodical E	N/A	8	120
Periodical F	---	8	120
Periodical G	N/A	8	120
Periodical H	N/A	8	120

Notes: The fewer the points in ranking the higher the rating--e.g., a ranking of 1 (non-weighted) and 15 (weighted) is the highest rating.

NA=Information on number of awards not available from periodical; periodical is assessed highest number of non-weighted points (8) and highest number of weighted points (15).

--periodical reports no awards garnered; periodical is assessed highest number of non-weighted points (8) and highest number of weighted points (15).

EDITORS WITH INDUSTRY-RELATED DEGREES AND/OR WORK EXPERIENCE

Table 12 compares the number of editors by periodical having industry-related degrees and/or work experience. Refer to the previous discussion in Chapter 1 on the rationale for treating degrees and work experience. While our hypothetical example (offshore oil) certainly requires a high degree of technical proficiency/knowledge in order to write the editorial articles that will appeal to, say, design engineers, the author does know of editors writing in the field who do not possess engineering degrees, but rather journalism degrees. These editors also have served in the offshore industry for a good number of years (ten year or more) and are able to "hold their own" when it comes to interviewing technical people and writing on technical subjects. Thus, for purposes of our hypothetical offshore oil example, these people are considered equivalent to editors with engineering degrees. The reader will have to evaluate his or her own particular situation and come to a decision as to how to rank the editors of the periodicals under study.

TABLE 12 EDITORS WITH INDUSTRY-RELATED DEGREES AND/OR WORK EXPERIENCE

Weighting: 15 points
Weighted Use Example: 1 (non-weighted ranking) x 15 points = 15

	Actual Degreed Editors And/Or Equivalent	Non-Weighted Ranking	Weighted Ranking
Periodical A	7	1	15
Periodical B	3	2	30
Periodical C	--	8	120
Periodical D	1	4	60
Periodical E	1	4	60
Periodical F	2	3	45
Periodical G	--	8	120
Periodical H	N/A	8	120

Notes: The fewer the points in ranking the higher the rating-- e.g., a ranking of 1 (non-weighted) and 15 (weighted) is the highest rating.

NA=Information on number of editors with industry related degrees or their work experience not available from periodical; periodical is assessed highest number of non-weighted points (8) and highest number of weighted points (120)

-- Periodical reports no industry-related degreed editors and its non-degreed editors all have less than ten years of industry-related work experience. Periodical is assessed highest number of non-weighted points (8) and highest number of weighted points (120).

It is interesting to note that periodical D and E are tied with the same number of industry-related degreed editors and thus share the fourth place position in the rankings.

READER SERVICE CARDS

Table 13 details the total number of individual reader service cards returned and processed from all issues published during the previous year of each periodical. As previously mentioned under the table discussion for editorial coverage of industry or field, when there is a mix of weeklies, semi-monthlies and/or bimonthlies with monthlies, the totals of each non-monthly must be averaged and adjusted in order to provide a fair comparison of the returns with those of the monthly periodicals.

TABLE 13. READER SERVICE CARDS

Weighting: 15 points
Weighted Use Example: 8 (non-weighted ranking) x 15 points = 120

	Actual Received	Non-Weighted Ranking	Weighted Ranking
Periodical A	10,651	1	15
Periodical B	8,768	3	45
Periodical C	5,146	5	75
Periodical D	8,405	4	60
Periodical E	1,473	6	90
Periodical F	8,933	2	30
Periodical G	788	7	105
Periodical H	N/A	8	120

Notes: The fewer the points in ranking the higher the rating--e.g., a ranking of 1 (non-weighted) and 15 (weighted) is the highest rating.

NA= Information on number of reader service cards returned not available from periodical; periodical is assessed highest number of non-weighted points (8) and highest number of weighted points (120).

ADVERTISING INQUIRIES RECEIVED

Table 14 reports the total number of inquiries received by each of the periodicals from all types of advertisements run during the previous 12 months. These inquiries are exclusive of any inquiries received directly by the advertiser via toll free 800 telemarketing numbers or from correspondence sent directly to the advertiser by the inquirer.

TABLE 14. ADVERTISING INQUIRIES RECEIVED

Weighting: <u>15 points</u>
Weighted Use Example: 5 (non-weighted ranking) x 15 points = 75

	Actual # Received	Non-Weighted Ranking	Weighted Ranking
Periodical A	14,780	1	15
Periodical B	12,801	3	45
Periodical C	9,200	5	75
Periodical D	13,300	2	30
Periodical E	4,375	6	90
Periodical F	12,600	4	60
Periodical G	1,050	7	105
Periodical H	N/A	8	120

Note: The fewer the points in ranking the higher the rating--e.g., a ranking of (non-weighted) and 15 (weighted) is the highest rating.

NA= Information on number of ad inquiries received not available from periodical; periodical is assessed highest number of non-weighted points (8) and highest number of weighted points (120).

One might ask "How can periodical A, for example, report 14,780 advertising inquiries received when it reported only 10,651 individual reader service cards returned?" One must remember that the format of the reader service card which the reader fills out and sends back to the periodical has provisions for requesting information on <u>ALL</u> ads and <u>ALL</u> editorial articles contained in the issue.

GENERAL EDITORIAL INQUIRIES RECEIVED

Table 15 presents the total number of inquiries received by each periodical that emanated from its editorial articles over the past 12 months. Note that in the main editorial will always out pull advertisements as it pertains to inquiries garnered.

31

TABLE 15. GENERAL EDITORIAL INQUIRIES

Weighting: <u>15 points</u>
Weighted Use Example: 6 (non-weighted ranking) x 15 points = 90

	Actual # Received	Non-Weighted Ranking	Weighted Ranking
Periodical A	35,900	1	15
Periodical B	20,175	4	60
Periodical C	12,445	5	75
Periodical D	27,200	3	45
Periodical E	8,500	6	90
Periodical F	34,250	2	30
Periodical G	3,500	7	105
Periodical H	N/A	8	120

Notes: The fewer the points in ranking the higher the rating--e.g., a ranking of 1 (non-weighted) and 15 (weighted) is the highest rating.

NA= Information on number of general editorial inquiries received not available from periodical; periodical is assessed the highest number of non-weighted points (8) and highest number of weighted points (120).

COST PER THOUSAND

The final key measurement category has to do with cost per thousand, i.e., what it costs to reach a thousand readers of each periodical with a black and white full page full run advertisement. Note: there is no reason why cost per thousand can't be figured on full color as long as the full color rate for each periodical is applied to all periodicals being measured.

TABLE 16. COST PER THOUSAND

Weighting: <u>15 points</u>
Weighted Use Example: 2 (non-weighted ranking) x 15 points = 30

	Actual Page Counts	Non-Weighted Ranking	Weighted Ranking
Periodical A	$379.20	3	45
Periodical B	$421.21	1	15
Periodical C	$207.79	5	75
Periodical D	$385.52	2	30
Periodical E	$199.89	6	90
Periodical F	$217.10	4	60
Periodical G	$176.29	7	105
Periodical H	$123.07	8	120

Note: The fewer the points in ranking the higher the rating--e.g., a ranking of 1 (non-weighted) and 15 (weighted) is the highest rating.

Why are the higher non-weighted rankings given to the higher costs per thousand in Table 16? Generally speaking, more value is promised when a higher cost is involved. However, the media planner is free to design his or her own value system to the consideration.

COMPOSITE NON-WEIGHTED AND WEIGHTED FINDINGS

Now that each of the hypothetical offshore oil periodicals has been ranked on a non-weighted and weighted basis on how well each did in the 15 key measurement categories, we need to rank each as to overall effectiveness in industry coverage according to the total scores achieved. To do this we first total the non-weighted points which each periodical achieved in each of the 15 categories (see Table 17.).

The total of the ranking numbers (from all of the measurement categories) is the periodical's total non-weighted score. For example, in Table 17 periodical B garnered 29 points which puts it in first place in the rankings. (Remember that the fewer the points the higher the rating.) Periodical A with 40 points comes in second and periodical F with 48 points comes in third.

Now let's see what happens to each periodical's ranking when the total of the weighted points is considered--see Table 18. Periodical B retains its first place position just as periodicals A and F remain in the second and third place positions, respectively, although the point spread is considerably more (101) on the weighted basis than it was on the non-weighted basis (8 points) for the latter two periodicals. But look what happened to periodical E. It moved up to sixth place on a weighted basis. (It was in eighth place on a non-weighted basis.) Also note that periodical G lost ground--going from seventh place (non-weighted) to eighth place (weighted); and periodical H also lost ground--going from sixth place (non-weighted) to seventh place (weighted). So weighting can make a difference as to how a publication fares in the rankings.

Using these tools just described, the media planner can systematically select the proper media for each individual advertising situation.

TABLE 17. SUMMARY OF FINDINGS--NON-WEIGHTED SCORES

Measurement Category	Periodicals							
	A	B	C	D	E	F	G	H
Total Circulation	1	2	5	6	4	3	7	8
Paid Circulation	8	1	8	2	4	3	8	8
Audited Circulation	1	1	1	1	1	1	8	1
Geographic Circulation	1	2	4	5	6	3	8	8
Circulation By Activity	1	2	5	4	6	3	7	8
Occupation/Job Function Circulation	1	2	8	4	5	3	8	8
Editorial Coverage of Industry/Field	4	1	8	2	7	3	6	5
Advertising Makeup	4	1	8	2	5	3	6	8
Editorial Makeup	4	2	6	1	7	3	8	5
# of Editorial Awards	8	2	1	8	8	8	8	8
Editors with Industry-Related Degrees and/or Work Experience	1	2	8	4	4	3	8	8
Reader Service Cards	1	3	5	4	6	2	7	8
Ad Inquiries Received	1	3	5	2	6	4	7	8
General Editorial Inquiries Received	1	4	5	3	6	2	7	8
Cost Per Thousand	3	1	5	2	6	4	7	7
TOTAL NON-WEIGHTED								
POINTS:	40	29	82	50	131	48	110	107
RANKING:	2	1	5	4	8	3	7	6

Note: The fewer the points the higher the ranking.

TABLE 18. SUMMARY OF FINDINGS--WEIGHTED SCORES

Measurement Category	A	B	C	D	E	F	G	H
Total Circulation	10	20	50	60	40	30	70	80
Paid Circulation	80	10	80	20	40	30	80	80
Audited Circulation	10	10	10	10	10	10	80	10
Geographic Circulation	10	20	40	50	60	30	80	80
Circulation By Activity	5	10	25	20	30	15	35	40
Occupation/Job Function Circulation	1	2	8	4	5	3	8	8
Editorial Coverage of Industry/Field	4	1	8	2	7	3	6	5
Advertising Makeup	40	10	80	20	50	30	60	80
Editorial Makeup	40	20	60	10	70	30	80	50
# of Editorial Awards	120	30	15	120	120	120	120	120
Editors with Industry- Related Degrees and/or Work Experience	15	30	120	60	60	45	120	120
Reader Service Cards	15	45	75	60	90	30	105	120
Ad Inquiries Received	15	45	75	30	90	60	105	120
General Editorial Inquiries Received	15	60	75	45	90	30	105	120
Cost Per Thousand	45	15	75	30	90	60	105	120
TOTAL WEIGHTED POINTS:	425	328	796	541	852	526	1159	1153
RANKING:	2	1	5	4	6	3	8	7

Note: The fewer the points the higher the ranking.

CHAPTER 4

SAMPLE MEASUREMENT TABLES

The following sample measurement tables contain the basic format used in the previous tables to illustrate the measurement and comparison techniques of each of the 15 key media selection considerations. These sample tables may be duplicated at will and are offered as an assist to the reader in organizing his or her media selection task.

TOTAL CIRCULATION

Weighting: _____ points
Weighted Use Example: Non-Weighted Ranking X Weighted Points = Weighted Ranking

Periodical Name	Actual/Total Circulation	Non-Weighted Ranking	Weighted Ranking
_____	_____	_____	_____
_____	_____	_____	_____
_____	_____	_____	_____
_____	_____	_____	_____
_____	_____	_____	_____
_____	_____	_____	_____
_____	_____	_____	_____
_____	_____	_____	_____
_____	_____	_____	_____
_____	_____	_____	_____
_____	_____	_____	_____
_____	_____	_____	_____
_____	_____	_____	_____

Note: The fewer the points in ranking the higher the rating.

PAID CIRCULATION

Weighting: _____ points
Weighted Use Example: Non-Weighted Ranking X Weighted Points = Weighted
Ranking

Periodical Name	Actual Paid Circulation	Non-Weighted Ranking	Weighted Ranking
_____	_____	_____	_____
_____	_____	_____	_____
_____	_____	_____	_____
_____	_____	_____	_____
_____	_____	_____	_____
_____	_____	_____	_____
_____	_____	_____	_____
_____	_____	_____	_____
_____	_____	_____	_____
_____	_____	_____	_____
_____	_____	_____	_____
_____	_____	_____	_____
_____	_____	_____	_____

Notes: The fewer the points in ranking the higher the rating.

Periodicals having no paid circulation or whose paid circulation figures are not available are assessed the highest number of non-weighted points and the highest weighted points.

AUDITED CIRCULATION

Weighting: _____ points
Weighted Use Example: Non-Weighted Ranking X Weighted Points = Weighted Ranking

Periodical Name	Actual Circulation	Non-Weighted Ranking	Weighted Ranking
_____	_____	_____	_____
_____	_____	_____	_____
_____	_____	_____	_____
_____	_____	_____	_____
_____	_____	_____	_____
_____	_____	_____	_____
_____	_____	_____	_____
_____	_____	_____	_____
_____	_____	_____	_____
_____	_____	_____	_____
_____	_____	_____	_____
_____	_____	_____	_____
_____	_____	_____	_____

Notes: The fewer the points in ranking the higher the rating.

Periodicals having no audited circulation or whose audited circulation figures are not available are assessed the highest number of non-weighted points and the highest weighted points.

GEOGRAPHIC CIRCULATION--_____
(Area)

Weighting: _____ points
Weighted Use Example: Non-Weighted Ranking X Weighted Points = Weighted Ranking

Periodical Name	Actual Circulation	Non-Weighted Ranking	Weighted Ranking
_____	_____	_____	_____
_____	_____	_____	_____
_____	_____	_____	_____
_____	_____	_____	_____
_____	_____	_____	_____
_____	_____	_____	_____
_____	_____	_____	_____
_____	_____	_____	_____
_____	_____	_____	_____
_____	_____	_____	_____
_____	_____	_____	_____
_____	_____	_____	_____
_____	_____	_____	_____
_____	_____	_____	_____

Note: The fewer the points in ranking the higher the rating.

Periodicals having no subject geographic circulation or whose subject geographic circulation figures are not available are assessed the highest number of non-weighted points and the highest weighted points.

CIRCULATION BY BUSINESS ACTIVITY--_____

(Type Industry)

Weighting: _____ points
Weighted Use Example: Non-Weighted Ranking X Weighted Points = Weighted Ranking

Periodical Name	Actual Circulation	Non-Weighted Ranking	Weighted Ranking
_____	_____	_____	_____
_____	_____	_____	_____
_____	_____	_____	_____
_____	_____	_____	_____
_____	_____	_____	_____
_____	_____	_____	_____
_____	_____	_____	_____
_____	_____	_____	_____
_____	_____	_____	_____
_____	_____	_____	_____
_____	_____	_____	_____
_____	_____	_____	_____
_____	_____	_____	_____

Notes: The fewer the points in ranking the higher the rating.

Periodicals having no such circulation or whose defined circulation figures are not available are assessed the highest number of non-weighted points and the highest weighted points.

CIRCULATION BY CONSUMER ACTIVITY--_____
(Demographic Type)

Weighting: _____ points
Weighted Use Example: Non-Weighted Ranking X Weighted Points = Weighted Ranking

Periodical Name	Actual Circulation	Non-Weighted Ranking	Weighted Ranking
_____	_____	_____	_____
_____	_____	_____	_____
_____	_____	_____	_____
_____	_____	_____	_____
_____	_____	_____	_____
_____	_____	_____	_____
_____	_____	_____	_____
_____	_____	_____	_____
_____	_____	_____	_____
_____	_____	_____	_____
_____	_____	_____	_____
_____	_____	_____	_____
_____	_____	_____	_____

Notes: The fewer the points in ranking the higher the rating.

Periodicals having no such demographic circulation or whose demographic circulation figures are not available are assessed the highest number of non-weighted points and the highest weighted points.

OCCUPATION/JOB FUNCTION CIRCULATION--_____
(Occupation or Job Function)

Weighting: _____ points

Weighted Use Example: Non-Weighted Ranking X Weighted Points = Weighted Ranking

Periodical Name	Actual Circulation	Non-Weighted Ranking	Weighted Ranking
_____	_____	_____	_____
_____	_____	_____	_____
_____	_____	_____	_____
_____	_____	_____	_____
_____	_____	_____	_____
_____	_____	_____	_____
_____	_____	_____	_____
_____	_____	_____	_____
_____	_____	_____	_____
_____	_____	_____	_____
_____	_____	_____	_____
_____	_____	_____	_____
_____	_____	_____	_____

Notes: The fewer the points in ranking the higher the rating.

Periodicals having no such occupation/job function circulation or whose defined circulation figures are not available are assessed the highest number of non-weighted points and the highest weighted points.

EDITORIAL COVERAGE OF--_____
_____(Type of Industry in General)

Weighting: _____ points
Weighted Use Example: Non-Weighted Ranking X Weighted Points = Weighted Ranking

Periodical Name	Actual Page Counts	Non-Weighted Ranking	Weighted Ranking
_____	_____	_____	_____
_____	_____	_____	_____
_____	_____	_____	_____
_____	_____	_____	_____
_____	_____	_____	_____
_____	_____	_____	_____
_____	_____	_____	_____
_____	_____	_____	_____
_____	_____	_____	_____
_____	_____	_____	_____
_____	_____	_____	_____
_____	_____	_____	_____
_____	_____	_____	_____

Notes: The fewer the points in ranking the higher the rating.

Periodicals having no such editorial pages devoted to subject or whose page counts are not available are assessed the highest number of non-weighted points and the highest weighted points.

ADVERTISING MAKEUP--_____
(Type of Product or Service)

Weighting: _____ points
Weighted Use Example: Non-Weighted Ranking X Weighted Points = Weighted Ranking

Periodical Name	Actual Page Counts	Non-Weighted Ranking	Weighted Ranking
_____	_____	_____	_____
_____	_____	_____	_____
_____	_____	_____	_____
_____	_____	_____	_____
_____	_____	_____	_____
_____	_____	_____	_____
_____	_____	_____	_____
_____	_____	_____	_____
_____	_____	_____	_____
_____	_____	_____	_____
_____	_____	_____	_____
_____	_____	_____	_____
_____	_____	_____	_____

Notes: The fewer the points in ranking the higher the rating.

Periodicals having no such ads devoted to subject or whose page counts are not available are assessed the highest number of non-weighted points and the highest weighted points.

EDITORIAL MAKEUP--_____
(Type of Product or Service)

Weighting: _____ points
Weighted Use Example: Non-Weighted Ranking X Weighted Points = Weighted Ranking

Periodical Name	Actual Page Counts	Non-Weighted Ranking	Weighted Ranking
_____	_____	_____	_____
_____	_____	_____	_____
_____	_____	_____	_____
_____	_____	_____	_____
_____	_____	_____	_____
_____	_____	_____	_____
_____	_____	_____	_____
_____	_____	_____	_____
_____	_____	_____	_____
_____	_____	_____	_____
_____	_____	_____	_____
_____	_____	_____	_____

Notes: The fewer the points in ranking the higher the rating.

Periodicals having no such editorial pages devoted to subject or whose page counts are not available are assessed the highest number of non-weighted points and the highest weighted points.

NUMBER OF EDITORIAL AWARDS

Weighting: _____ points

Weighted Use Example: Non-Weighted Ranking X Weighted Points = Weighted Ranking

Periodical Name	Actual # Awarded	Non-Weighted Ranking	Weighted Ranking
_____	_____	_____	_____
_____	_____	_____	_____
_____	_____	_____	_____
_____	_____	_____	_____
_____	_____	_____	_____
_____	_____	_____	_____
_____	_____	_____	_____
_____	_____	_____	_____
_____	_____	_____	_____
_____	_____	_____	_____
_____	_____	_____	_____
_____	_____	_____	_____

Notes: The fewer the points in ranking the higher the rating.

Periodicals having no awards to report or whose award numbers are not available are assessed the highest number of non-weighted points and the highest weighted points.

EDITORS WITH INDUSTRY-RELATED DEGREES
AND/OR EXPERIENCE

Weighting: _____ points
Weighted Use Example: Non-Weighted Ranking X Weighted Points = Weighted Ranking

Periodical Name	Actual Degreed Editors &/or Equivalent	Non-Weighted Ranking	Weighted Ranking

Notes: The fewer the points in ranking the higher the rating.

Periodicals having no industry-related degreed editors and no non-degreed editors with 10 years or more of industry-related experience or whose information on same is not available are assessed the highest number of non-weighted points and highest weighted points.

READER SERVICE CARDS

Weighting: _____ points

Weighted Use Example: Non-Weighted Ranking X Weighted Points = Weighted Ranking

Periodical Name	Actual # Returned	Non-Weighted Ranking	Weighted Ranking
_____	_____	_____	_____
_____	_____	_____	_____
_____	_____	_____	_____
_____	_____	_____	_____
_____	_____	_____	_____
_____	_____	_____	_____
_____	_____	_____	_____
_____	_____	_____	_____
_____	_____	_____	_____
_____	_____	_____	_____
_____	_____	_____	_____
_____	_____	_____	_____

Notes: The fewer the points in ranking the higher the rating.

Periodicals having no returned reader service cards to report or which do not make such information on returned cards available are assessed the highest number of non-weighted points and the highest weighted points.

ADVERTISING INQUIRIES RECEIVED

Weighting: _____ points

Weighted Use Example: Non-Weighted Ranking X Weighted Points = Weighted Ranking

Periodical Name	Actual # Received	Non-Weighted Ranking	Weighted Ranking

Notes: The fewer the points in ranking the higher the rating.

Periodicals having no advertising inquiries to report or which do not make such information available on advertising inquiries are assessed the highest number of non-weighted points and the highest weighted points.

51

GENERAL EDITORIAL INQUIRIES RECEIVED

Weighting: _____ points

Weighted Use Example: Non-Weighted Ranking X Weighted Points = Weighted Ranking

Periodical Name	Actual # Received	Non-Weighted Ranking	Weighted Ranking
_____	_____	_____	_____
_____	_____	_____	_____
_____	_____	_____	_____
_____	_____	_____	_____
_____	_____	_____	_____
_____	_____	_____	_____
_____	_____	_____	_____
_____	_____	_____	_____
_____	_____	_____	_____
_____	_____	_____	_____
_____	_____	_____	_____
_____	_____	_____	_____

Notes: The fewer the points in ranking the higher the rating.

Periodicals having no general editorial inquiries to report or which do not make such information available are assessed the highest number of non-weighted points and the highest weighted points.

COST PER THOUSAND

Weighting: _____ points

Weighted Use Example: Non-Weighted Ranking X Weighted Points = Weighted Ranking

Periodical Name	Actual Cost	Non-Weighted Ranking	Weighted Ranking
_____	_____	_____	_____
_____	_____	_____	_____
_____	_____	_____	_____
_____	_____	_____	_____
_____	_____	_____	_____
_____	_____	_____	_____
_____	_____	_____	_____
_____	_____	_____	_____
_____	_____	_____	_____
_____	_____	_____	_____
_____	_____	_____	_____
_____	_____	_____	_____

Note: The fewer the points in ranking the higher the rating.

SUMMARY OF FINDINGS--NON-WEIGHTED SCORES

Measurement Category	Periodicals							
	A	B	C	D	E	F	G	H
Total Circulation	—	—	—	—	—	—	—	—
Paid Circulation	—	—	—	—	—	—	—	—
Audited Circulation	—	—	—	—	—	—	—	—
Geographic Circulation	—	—	—	—	—	—	—	—
Circulation By Activity	—	—	—	—	—	—	—	—
Occupation/Job Function Circulation	—	—	—	—	—	—	—	—
Editorial Coverage of Industry/Field	—	—	—	—	—	—	—	—
Advertising Makeup	—	—	—	—	—	—	—	—
Editorial Makeup	—	—	—	—	—	—	—	—
# of Editorial Awards	—	—	—	—	—	—	—	—
Editors with Industry-Related Degrees and/or Work Experience	—	—	—	—	—	—	—	—
Reader Service Cards	—	—	—	—	—	—	—	—
Ad Inquiries Received	—	—	—	—	—	—	—	—
General Editorial Inquiries Received	—	—	—	—	—	—	—	—
Cost Per Thousand	—	—	—	—	—	—	—	—
TOTAL NON-WEIGHTED POINTS:	—	—	—	—	—	—	—	—
RANKING:	—	—	—	—	—	—	—	—

Note: The fewer the points the higher the ranking.

SUMMARY OF FINDINGS--WEIGHTED SCORES

Measurement Category	Periodicals							
	A	B	C	D	E	F	G	H
Total Circulation	—	—	—	—	—	—	—	—
Paid Circulation	—	—	—	—	—	—	—	—
Audited Circulation	—	—	—	—	—	—	—	—
Geographic Circulation	—	—	—	—	—	—	—	—
Circulation By Activity	—	—	—	—	—	—	—	—
Occupation/Job Function Circulation	—	—	—	—	—	—	—	—
Editorial Coverage of Industry/Field	—	—	—	—	—	—	—	—
Advertising Makeup	—	—	—	—	—	—	—	—
Editorial Makeup	—	—	—	—	—	—	—	—
# of Editorial Awards	—	—	—	—	—	—	—	—
Editors with Industry-Related Degrees and/or Work Experience	—	—	—	—	—	—	—	—
Reader Service Cards	—	—	—	—	—	—	—	—
Ad Inquiries Received	—	—	—	—	—	—	—	—
General Editorial Inquiries Received	—	—	—	—	—	—	—	—
Cost Per Thousand	—	—	—	—	—	—	—	—
TOTAL NON-WEIGHTED POINTS:	—	—	—	—	—	—	—	—
RANKING:	—	—	—	—	—	—	—	—

Note: The fewer the points the higher the ranking.

INDEX

FOR MORE INFORMATION
Print media planning books by R.L. Ehler

Print Media Planning Manual--A complete practical guide to preparing a media plan and buying space for periodical advertising. Takes the reader step by step through the media processes including [] finding direction for the planning process [] budgeting expenditures [] negotiating with periodicals [] targeting the right audiences [] setting appropriate objectives and measuring performance [] using different media in one plan [] profiling competing periodicals [] sources for media facts and figures [] analyzing pros and cons of each medium [] mapping tactics and strategies [] scheduling ad appearances [] presenting the media plan [] following through after placement [] trade customs and practices [] organizing a media operation [] media terms and their definitions.

Directory of Print Media Advertising Resources--A comprehensive directory listing the names, addresses and telephone numbers of virtually every important source for facts and figures about periodicals, organizations and services--both in the United States and abroad--which are available to the print media advertiser, planner and buyer. Extensive description of resource content/service provided also included for most listings.

Media Analysis Tools--A set of tools that allow the advertising media planner to systematically measure and compare on a numerical basis the various attributes of competing periodicals in a given advertising situation. These tools can be an indispensable aid to making sound decisions concerning media selection since they allow the media planner to examine the most crucial aspects of a publication's worth to the advertiser.

Checklists for Print Media Advertising Planning and Buying--13 basic checklists, 195 specific things to check when planning and buying advertising in periodicals. These handy checklists cover all of the considerations that the media planner needs to make when preparing a media plan and buying space for periodical advertising.

Request FREE descriptive brochure from Richler & Co.

ORDER FORM

RICHLER & CO
754 Palermo Dr., Ste. A
Santa Barbara, CA 93105 U.S.A.
Phone (805) 569-1668
FAX (805) 569-2279

Please send me the following books by R.L. Ehler:

_____copies of Print Media Planning Manual @ $49.95 each.
_____copies of Directory of Print Media Advertising Resources @ $44.95 each.
_____copies of Media Analysis Tools @ $34.95 each.
_____copies of Checklists for Print Media Advertising Planning & Buying @ $19.95 each.

I understand that I may return any book for a full refund if not satisfied.

Name: _____
Address: _____
_____ZIP _____

Californians: Please add $7.75% sales tax.

Shipping: $2.00 for the first book and .75 cents for each additional book.

_____I can't wait 3-4 weeks for Book Rate Shipment. Here is $3.50 per book for Air
Mail.

ORDER FORM

RICHLER & CO
754 Palermo Dr., Ste. A
Santa Barbara, CA 93105 U.S.A.
Phone   (805) 569-1668
FAX   (805) 569-2279

Please send me the following books by R.L. Ehler:

_____copies of Print Media Planning Manual @ $49.95 each.
_____copies of Directory of Print Media Advertising Resources @ $44.95 each.
_____copies of Media Analysis Tools @ $34.95 each.
_____copies of Checklists for Print Media Advertising Planning & Buying @ $19.95 each.

I understand that I may return any book for a full refund if not satisfied.

Name: _____
Address: _____
_____ZIP _____

Californians: Please add 7.75% sales tax.

Shipping: $2.25 for the first book and $1.00 for each additional book.

_____I can't wait 3-4 weeks for Book Rate Shipment. Here is $3.50 per book for Air Mail.